50 Perfect Pies for Home

By: Kelly Johnson

Table of Contents

- Classic Apple Pie
- Pumpkin Pie
- Pecan Pie
- Cherry Pie
- Blueberry Pie
- Lemon Meringue Pie
- Key Lime Pie
- Chocolate Cream Pie
- Banana Cream Pie
- Sweet Potato Pie
- Peach Pie
- Strawberry Rhubarb Pie
- Coconut Cream Pie
- French Silk Pie
- Strawberry Pie
- Mixed Berry Pie
- Coconut Custard Pie
- Chocolate Peanut Butter Pie
- Pineapple Coconut Pie
- Black Bottom Pie
- S'mores Pie
- Chocolate Chess Pie
- Buttermilk Pie
- Maple Pecan Pie
- Almond Joy Pie
- Apple Cranberry Pie
- Raspberry Pie
- Triple Berry Pie
- Grasshopper Pie
- Lemon Icebox Pie
- Apricot Pie
- Mango Pie
- Maple Pumpkin Pie
- Maple Bacon Pie
- Bourbon Pecan Pie

- Bourbon Chocolate Pecan Pie
- Cinnamon Roll Pie
- Caramel Apple Pie
- Chocolate Caramel Pie
- Apple Pear Pie
- Blackberry Pie
- Pineapple Mango Pie
- Pear Ginger Pie
- Lime Coconut Pie
- Chiffon Pie
- Chocolate Hazelnut Pie
- Cranberry Orange Pie
- Spiced Pear Pie
- Chocolate Almond Pie
- Butterscotch Pie

Classic Apple Pie

Ingredients:

- 6 cups sliced apples (Granny Smith or Honeycrisp)
- 1 tablespoon lemon juice
- 3/4 cup granulated sugar
- 1/4 cup brown sugar
- 1 teaspoon cinnamon
- 1/4 teaspoon nutmeg
- 2 tablespoons flour
- 1 tablespoon butter, cubed
- 1 package pie crusts (or homemade crust)

Instructions:

1. Preheat the oven to 375°F (190°C).
2. In a large bowl, toss the apple slices with lemon juice, granulated sugar, brown sugar, cinnamon, nutmeg, and flour.
3. Roll out the pie crust and fit it into a pie pan. Pour the apple mixture into the crust and dot with butter.
4. Top with the second pie crust, crimping the edges to seal. Cut a few slits in the top crust for ventilation.
5. Bake for 45-50 minutes until the crust is golden and the filling is bubbly. Let cool before serving.

Pumpkin Pie

Ingredients:

- 1 can (15 oz) pumpkin puree
- 3/4 cup heavy cream
- 1/2 cup brown sugar
- 2 large eggs
- 1 teaspoon cinnamon
- 1/2 teaspoon ground ginger
- 1/4 teaspoon nutmeg
- 1/4 teaspoon salt
- 1 teaspoon vanilla extract
- 1 package pie crust (or homemade crust)

Instructions:

1. Preheat the oven to 375°F (190°C).
2. In a bowl, whisk together pumpkin puree, heavy cream, brown sugar, eggs, cinnamon, ginger, nutmeg, salt, and vanilla extract until smooth.
3. Pour the pumpkin mixture into the pie crust.
4. Bake for 45-50 minutes until the center is set and a knife inserted comes out clean.
5. Let cool before serving. Optionally, top with whipped cream.

Pecan Pie

Ingredients:

- 1 1/2 cups pecans, chopped
- 3/4 cup light corn syrup
- 1/2 cup granulated sugar
- 1/4 cup brown sugar
- 3 large eggs
- 1/4 cup melted butter
- 1 teaspoon vanilla extract
- 1 package pie crust (or homemade crust)

Instructions:

1. Preheat the oven to 350°F (175°C).
2. In a bowl, whisk together corn syrup, granulated sugar, brown sugar, eggs, melted butter, and vanilla extract.
3. Stir in chopped pecans.
4. Pour the filling into the pie crust and bake for 45-50 minutes until the filling is set and slightly puffed.
5. Let cool before serving.

Cherry Pie

Ingredients:

- 4 cups fresh or frozen cherries, pitted
- 3/4 cup granulated sugar
- 1 tablespoon lemon juice
- 1 tablespoon cornstarch
- 1 package pie crust (or homemade crust)

Instructions:

1. Preheat the oven to 375°F (190°C).
2. In a bowl, combine cherries, sugar, lemon juice, and cornstarch. Mix until the fruit is coated.
3. Roll out the pie crust and fit it into a pie pan. Pour the cherry mixture into the crust.
4. Top with the second crust, crimp the edges, and cut slits in the top for ventilation.
5. Bake for 45-50 minutes until the crust is golden and the filling is bubbly.
6. Let cool before serving.

Blueberry Pie

Ingredients:

- 4 cups fresh or frozen blueberries
- 3/4 cup granulated sugar
- 2 tablespoons cornstarch
- 1 tablespoon lemon juice
- 1/4 teaspoon cinnamon
- 1 package pie crust (or homemade crust)

Instructions:

1. Preheat the oven to 375°F (190°C).
2. In a bowl, mix blueberries, sugar, cornstarch, lemon juice, and cinnamon.
3. Roll out the pie crust and fit it into a pie pan. Pour the blueberry mixture into the crust.
4. Top with the second crust, crimp the edges, and cut slits in the top for ventilation.
5. Bake for 45-50 minutes until the crust is golden and the filling is bubbly.
6. Let cool before serving.

Lemon Meringue Pie

Ingredients for Filling:

- 1 1/2 cups water
- 1 cup granulated sugar
- 1/4 cup cornstarch
- 1/4 teaspoon salt
- 4 large egg yolks, beaten
- 1/2 cup fresh lemon juice
- 1 tablespoon lemon zest
- 2 tablespoons butter

For Meringue:

- 4 large egg whites
- 1/4 teaspoon cream of tartar
- 1/4 cup granulated sugar

Instructions:

1. Preheat the oven to 350°F (175°C).
2. In a saucepan, combine water, sugar, cornstarch, and salt. Bring to a boil, stirring constantly, until thickened.
3. Remove from heat and gradually whisk in the egg yolks. Stir in lemon juice, lemon zest, and butter until smooth.
4. Pour the filling into the pre-baked pie crust.
5. For the meringue, beat egg whites and cream of tartar until soft peaks form. Gradually add sugar, continuing to beat until stiff peaks form.
6. Spread the meringue over the pie, sealing the edges.
7. Bake for 10-12 minutes until the meringue is golden brown. Let cool before serving.

Key Lime Pie

Ingredients:

- 1 can (14 oz) sweetened condensed milk
- 1/2 cup fresh key lime juice
- 2 large egg yolks
- 1 pre-baked graham cracker crust
- Whipped cream for topping (optional)

Instructions:

1. Preheat the oven to 350°F (175°C).
2. In a bowl, whisk together sweetened condensed milk, lime juice, and egg yolks.
3. Pour the mixture into the graham cracker crust.
4. Bake for 15-20 minutes until set.
5. Let cool before refrigerating for at least 2 hours. Top with whipped cream before serving.

Chocolate Cream Pie

Ingredients:

- 1 pre-baked pie crust
- 1 1/2 cups heavy cream
- 3/4 cup granulated sugar
- 1/4 cup cocoa powder
- 2 tablespoons cornstarch
- 1/4 teaspoon salt
- 4 large egg yolks
- 2 tablespoons butter
- 1 teaspoon vanilla extract

Instructions:

1. In a saucepan, whisk together sugar, cocoa powder, cornstarch, and salt.
2. Gradually whisk in heavy cream and cook over medium heat, stirring constantly, until the mixture thickens.
3. Remove from heat and whisk in egg yolks, butter, and vanilla extract until smooth.
4. Pour the filling into the pre-baked pie crust and chill for 4 hours.
5. Top with whipped cream and serve.

Banana Cream Pie

Ingredients:

- 2-3 ripe bananas, sliced
- 1 pre-baked pie crust
- 2 cups heavy cream
- 1/2 cup granulated sugar
- 1/4 cup cornstarch
- 1/4 teaspoon salt
- 4 large egg yolks
- 1 teaspoon vanilla extract

Instructions:

1. In a saucepan, combine sugar, cornstarch, and salt. Gradually whisk in heavy cream and cook over medium heat until thickened.
2. Remove from heat and whisk in egg yolks and vanilla extract.
3. Layer the bottom of the pre-baked pie crust with sliced bananas, then pour the cream mixture over the top.
4. Chill for 4 hours and top with whipped cream before serving.

Sweet Potato Pie

Ingredients:

- 2 cups mashed cooked sweet potatoes
- 1 cup granulated sugar
- 1/2 cup evaporated milk
- 2 large eggs
- 1 teaspoon vanilla extract
- 1 teaspoon cinnamon
- 1/2 teaspoon nutmeg
- 1/4 teaspoon ground ginger
- 1/4 teaspoon salt
- 1 pre-baked pie crust

Instructions:

1. Preheat the oven to 375°F (190°C).
2. In a bowl, combine mashed sweet potatoes, sugar, evaporated milk, eggs, vanilla extract, cinnamon, nutmeg, ginger, and salt. Mix until smooth.
3. Pour the mixture into the pre-baked pie crust.
4. Bake for 40-45 minutes until set and the top is golden. Let cool before serving.

Peach Pie

Ingredients:

- 4 cups fresh or frozen peaches, sliced
- 3/4 cup granulated sugar
- 1 tablespoon lemon juice
- 1/4 teaspoon ground cinnamon
- 2 tablespoons cornstarch
- 1 package pie crust (or homemade crust)

Instructions:

1. Preheat the oven to 375°F (190°C).
2. In a bowl, combine peaches, sugar, lemon juice, cinnamon, and cornstarch. Toss until evenly coated.
3. Roll out the pie crust and fit it into a pie pan. Pour the peach mixture into the crust.
4. Top with the second pie crust, crimp the edges, and cut slits in the top for ventilation.
5. Bake for 45-50 minutes until the crust is golden and the filling is bubbly. Let cool before serving.

Strawberry Rhubarb Pie

Ingredients:

- 2 cups fresh strawberries, sliced
- 2 cups rhubarb, chopped
- 1 1/4 cups granulated sugar
- 1/4 cup cornstarch
- 1 tablespoon lemon juice
- 1/4 teaspoon salt
- 1 package pie crust (or homemade crust)

Instructions:

1. Preheat the oven to 375°F (190°C).
2. In a bowl, mix strawberries, rhubarb, sugar, cornstarch, lemon juice, and salt.
3. Roll out the pie crust and place in a pie pan. Pour the strawberry-rhubarb mixture into the crust.
4. Top with a second crust, crimp the edges, and cut slits for ventilation.
5. Bake for 45-50 minutes until the crust is golden and the filling is bubbly. Let cool before serving.

Coconut Cream Pie

Ingredients for Filling:

- 1 can (13.5 oz) coconut milk
- 1 1/2 cups heavy cream
- 1/2 cup granulated sugar
- 1/4 cup cornstarch
- 4 large egg yolks
- 1/2 teaspoon vanilla extract
- 1 1/2 cups shredded coconut, toasted

For Meringue:

- 4 large egg whites
- 1/4 teaspoon cream of tartar
- 1/4 cup granulated sugar

Instructions:

1. Preheat the oven to 350°F (175°C). In a saucepan, whisk together coconut milk, heavy cream, sugar, and cornstarch.
2. Cook over medium heat, whisking constantly, until the mixture thickens.
3. Beat the egg yolks and gradually add a little of the hot mixture to temper them. Add the egg mixture back into the saucepan and cook for another 2-3 minutes.
4. Stir in vanilla extract and toasted coconut. Pour into a pre-baked pie crust.
5. For the meringue, beat egg whites and cream of tartar until soft peaks form. Gradually add sugar and beat until stiff peaks form.
6. Spread meringue over the pie and bake for 10-12 minutes until golden. Let cool before serving.

French Silk Pie

Ingredients for Filling:

- 1/2 cup unsalted butter, softened
- 1 cup granulated sugar
- 4 oz semi-sweet chocolate, melted
- 2 teaspoons vanilla extract
- 2 large eggs
- 1 1/2 cups whipped cream

For Whipped Cream Topping:

- 1 cup heavy cream
- 2 tablespoons powdered sugar
- 1/2 teaspoon vanilla extract

Instructions:

1. Beat the butter and sugar in a bowl until light and fluffy. Add melted chocolate and vanilla extract.
2. Beat in the eggs one at a time, mixing well after each addition. Continue beating for 5 minutes until fluffy and smooth.
3. Pour the filling into a pre-baked pie crust. Refrigerate for at least 4 hours.
4. Whip the cream with powdered sugar and vanilla until stiff peaks form. Spread over the pie before serving.

Strawberry Pie

Ingredients:

- 4 cups fresh strawberries, sliced
- 1 cup granulated sugar
- 1/4 cup cornstarch
- 1/2 cup water
- 1 tablespoon lemon juice
- 1 package pie crust (or homemade crust)

Instructions:

1. Preheat the oven to 375°F (190°C). Roll out the pie crust and place it in a pie pan.
2. In a saucepan, combine sugar, cornstarch, water, and lemon juice. Cook over medium heat until thickened and clear.
3. Stir in the sliced strawberries, then pour the filling into the pie crust.
4. Bake for 25-30 minutes until the crust is golden and the filling is set. Let cool before serving.

Mixed Berry Pie

Ingredients:

- 3 cups mixed berries (blueberries, raspberries, blackberries, strawberries)
- 3/4 cup granulated sugar
- 1/4 cup cornstarch
- 1 tablespoon lemon juice
- 1 package pie crust (or homemade crust)

Instructions:

1. Preheat the oven to 375°F (190°C). In a bowl, mix berries, sugar, cornstarch, and lemon juice.
2. Roll out the pie crust and place in a pie pan. Pour the berry mixture into the crust.
3. Top with a second pie crust, crimp the edges, and cut slits in the top for ventilation.
4. Bake for 45-50 minutes until the crust is golden and the filling is bubbly. Let cool before serving.

Coconut Custard Pie

Ingredients:

- 1 can (13.5 oz) coconut milk
- 1 cup heavy cream
- 3/4 cup granulated sugar
- 3 large eggs
- 1 teaspoon vanilla extract
- 1 1/2 cups shredded coconut

Instructions:

1. Preheat the oven to 350°F (175°C).
2. In a bowl, whisk together coconut milk, heavy cream, sugar, eggs, and vanilla extract.
3. Stir in shredded coconut.
4. Pour the mixture into a pre-baked pie crust and bake for 40-45 minutes until set.
5. Let cool before serving.

Chocolate Peanut Butter Pie

Ingredients:

- 1 package graham cracker crust
- 1 cup creamy peanut butter
- 1/2 cup powdered sugar
- 1 package (8 oz) cream cheese, softened
- 1 cup heavy cream
- 1/2 cup semi-sweet chocolate chips

Instructions:

1. In a bowl, mix peanut butter, powdered sugar, and cream cheese until smooth.
2. Whip the heavy cream until stiff peaks form, then fold it into the peanut butter mixture.
3. Pour the filling into the graham cracker crust.
4. Melt the chocolate chips and drizzle over the pie.
5. Refrigerate for at least 4 hours before serving.

Pineapple Coconut Pie

Ingredients:

- 1 can (15 oz) crushed pineapple, drained
- 1 1/2 cups shredded coconut
- 1/2 cup granulated sugar
- 2 eggs, beaten
- 1 tablespoon flour
- 1 package pie crust (or homemade crust)

Instructions:

1. Preheat the oven to 375°F (190°C).
2. In a bowl, mix pineapple, coconut, sugar, eggs, and flour until combined.
3. Pour the mixture into a pre-baked pie crust.
4. Bake for 30-35 minutes until the top is golden. Let cool before serving.

Black Bottom Pie

Ingredients for Bottom Layer:

- 1/2 cup semi-sweet chocolate chips
- 1 tablespoon butter

For Top Layer:

- 1 package (8 oz) cream cheese, softened
- 1 cup powdered sugar
- 1 cup whipped cream
- 1 teaspoon vanilla extract

Instructions:

1. In a small saucepan, melt chocolate chips and butter over low heat. Pour into the bottom of a pre-baked pie crust and refrigerate until set.
2. In a bowl, beat cream cheese and powdered sugar until smooth. Fold in whipped cream and vanilla extract.
3. Spread the cream cheese mixture over the chocolate layer and refrigerate for at least 2 hours before serving.

S'mores Pie

Ingredients:

- 1 graham cracker crust
- 1 cup semi-sweet chocolate chips
- 1 cup heavy cream
- 2 cups mini marshmallows
- 1 tablespoon butter

Instructions:

1. Preheat the oven to 350°F (175°C). In a saucepan, heat heavy cream until just simmering. Pour over chocolate chips and butter. Stir until smooth.
2. Pour the chocolate mixture into the graham cracker crust and refrigerate for 1 hour to set.
3. Top with mini marshmallows and bake for 2-3 minutes until the marshmallows are golden brown. Let cool before serving.

Chocolate Chess Pie

Ingredients:

- 1 1/2 cups granulated sugar
- 1/2 cup unsweetened cocoa powder
- 1/4 teaspoon salt
- 3 large eggs
- 1/2 cup unsalted butter, melted
- 1 teaspoon vanilla extract
- 1 package pie crust (or homemade crust)

Instructions:

1. Preheat the oven to 350°F (175°C).
2. In a bowl, whisk together sugar, cocoa powder, and salt. Add eggs, melted butter, and vanilla extract, mixing until smooth.
3. Pour the filling into a pre-baked pie crust and bake for 40-45 minutes until the center is set.
4. Let cool before serving.

Buttermilk Pie

Ingredients:

- 1 1/2 cups buttermilk
- 1 1/2 cups granulated sugar
- 1/4 cup melted butter
- 3 large eggs
- 2 tablespoons all-purpose flour
- 1 teaspoon vanilla extract
- 1/4 teaspoon salt
- 1 package pie crust (or homemade crust)

Instructions:

1. Preheat the oven to 350°F (175°C). In a bowl, whisk together buttermilk, sugar, melted butter, eggs, flour, vanilla extract, and salt until smooth.
2. Pour the mixture into the pre-baked pie crust.
3. Bake for 45-50 minutes until the filling is set and the top is lightly golden.
4. Let cool completely before serving.

Maple Pecan Pie

Ingredients:

- 1 1/2 cups pecan halves
- 1/2 cup maple syrup
- 1/2 cup light corn syrup
- 1/4 cup brown sugar
- 1/4 cup melted butter
- 3 large eggs
- 1 teaspoon vanilla extract
- 1 package pie crust (or homemade crust)

Instructions:

1. Preheat the oven to 350°F (175°C). In a bowl, combine maple syrup, corn syrup, brown sugar, melted butter, eggs, and vanilla extract. Mix until smooth.
2. Stir in the pecans and pour the mixture into the pre-baked pie crust.
3. Bake for 45-50 minutes until the pie is set and the top is golden. Let cool before serving.

Almond Joy Pie

Ingredients:

- 1 package pie crust (or homemade crust)
- 1 1/2 cups shredded coconut
- 1 cup milk chocolate chips
- 1/2 cup whole almonds
- 3/4 cup heavy cream
- 1/4 cup sweetened condensed milk
- 1/4 cup sugar
- 1 teaspoon vanilla extract

Instructions:

1. Preheat the oven to 350°F (175°C). In a bowl, mix shredded coconut, milk chocolate chips, and almonds.
2. Pour the mixture into the pre-baked pie crust.
3. In another bowl, whisk together heavy cream, sweetened condensed milk, sugar, and vanilla extract. Pour over the coconut mixture.
4. Bake for 30-35 minutes until the top is golden and the filling is set. Let cool before serving.

Apple Cranberry Pie

Ingredients:

- 4 cups peeled and sliced apples (Granny Smith or Honeycrisp)
- 1 cup fresh or frozen cranberries
- 3/4 cup granulated sugar
- 1/4 cup brown sugar
- 1 teaspoon cinnamon
- 1 tablespoon lemon juice
- 1 tablespoon cornstarch
- 1 package pie crust (or homemade crust)

Instructions:

1. Preheat the oven to 375°F (190°C). In a bowl, mix apples, cranberries, granulated sugar, brown sugar, cinnamon, lemon juice, and cornstarch.
2. Roll out the pie crust and place it in a pie pan. Pour the apple-cranberry mixture into the crust.
3. Top with a second crust, crimp the edges, and cut slits in the top for ventilation.
4. Bake for 45-50 minutes until the crust is golden and the filling is bubbly. Let cool before serving.

Raspberry Pie

Ingredients:

- 4 cups fresh or frozen raspberries
- 3/4 cup granulated sugar
- 2 tablespoons cornstarch
- 1 tablespoon lemon juice
- 1 package pie crust (or homemade crust)

Instructions:

1. Preheat the oven to 375°F (190°C). In a bowl, mix raspberries, sugar, cornstarch, and lemon juice.
2. Roll out the pie crust and place it in a pie pan. Pour the raspberry mixture into the crust.
3. Top with a second crust, crimp the edges, and cut slits in the top for ventilation.
4. Bake for 45-50 minutes until the crust is golden and the filling is bubbly. Let cool before serving

Triple Berry Pie

Ingredients:

- 2 cups strawberries, sliced
- 1 cup blueberries
- 1 cup raspberries
- 1 cup granulated sugar
- 2 tablespoons cornstarch
- 1 tablespoon lemon juice
- 1 package pie crust (or homemade crust)

Instructions:

1. Preheat the oven to 375°F (190°C). In a bowl, combine strawberries, blueberries, raspberries, sugar, cornstarch, and lemon juice.
2. Roll out the pie crust and place it in a pie pan. Pour the berry mixture into the crust.
3. Top with a second crust, crimp the edges, and cut slits in the top for ventilation.
4. Bake for 45-50 minutes until the crust is golden and the filling is bubbly. Let cool before serving.

Grasshopper Pie

Ingredients:

- 1 pre-baked chocolate pie crust
- 1 1/2 cups heavy cream
- 1/2 cup mint chocolate chips
- 1/4 cup green crème de menthe
- 1/4 cup white crème de cacao
- 1/2 cup powdered sugar

Instructions:

1. In a saucepan, heat the heavy cream until warm. Stir in mint chocolate chips and whisk until smooth.
2. Remove from heat and stir in crème de menthe and crème de cacao. Cool to room temperature.
3. In a bowl, beat powdered sugar into the cream mixture. Pour into the pre-baked pie crust.
4. Chill for 4 hours or until set. Serve with whipped cream on top if desired.

Lemon Icebox Pie

Ingredients:

- 1 package graham cracker crust
- 1 can (14 oz) sweetened condensed milk
- 1/2 cup fresh lemon juice
- 2 large egg yolks
- 1/2 teaspoon vanilla extract

Instructions:

1. Preheat the oven to 350°F (175°C). In a bowl, whisk together sweetened condensed milk, lemon juice, egg yolks, and vanilla extract.
2. Pour the mixture into the graham cracker crust and bake for 15 minutes until set.
3. Let cool and refrigerate for at least 2 hours before serving.

Apricot Pie

Ingredients:

- 4 cups fresh or dried apricots, chopped
- 1 cup granulated sugar
- 1 tablespoon lemon juice
- 1 tablespoon cornstarch
- 1 package pie crust (or homemade crust)

Instructions:

1. Preheat the oven to 375°F (190°C). In a bowl, mix apricots, sugar, lemon juice, and cornstarch.
2. Roll out the pie crust and place it in a pie pan. Pour the apricot mixture into the crust.
3. Top with a second crust, crimp the edges, and cut slits in the top for ventilation.
4. Bake for 45-50 minutes until the crust is golden and the filling is bubbly. Let cool before serving.

Mango Pie

Ingredients:

- 2 ripe mangoes, peeled and chopped
- 1/2 cup granulated sugar
- 2 tablespoons lime juice
- 1 tablespoon cornstarch
- 1/4 teaspoon salt
- 1 package pie crust (or homemade crust)

Instructions:

1. Preheat the oven to 375°F (190°C). In a bowl, mix mangoes, sugar, lime juice, cornstarch, and salt.
2. Roll out the pie crust and place it in a pie pan. Pour the mango mixture into the crust.
3. Top with a second crust, crimp the edges, and cut slits in the top for ventilation.
4. Bake for 40-45 minutes until the crust is golden and the filling is bubbly. Let cool before serving.

Maple Pumpkin Pie

Ingredients:

- 1 can (15 oz) pumpkin puree
- 3/4 cup maple syrup
- 1/2 cup heavy cream
- 2 large eggs
- 1 teaspoon cinnamon
- 1/2 teaspoon nutmeg
- 1/4 teaspoon ground ginger
- 1/4 teaspoon salt
- 1 package pie crust (or homemade crust)

Instructions:

1. Preheat the oven to 375°F (190°C).
2. In a bowl, whisk together pumpkin puree, maple syrup, heavy cream, eggs, cinnamon, nutmeg, ginger, and salt until smooth.
3. Pour the mixture into the pre-baked pie crust.
4. Bake for 45-50 minutes until the filling is set and the top is slightly golden.
5. Let cool before serving.

Maple Bacon Pie

Ingredients:

- 1 package pie crust (or homemade crust)
- 1 cup cooked bacon, crumbled
- 1 cup maple syrup
- 1/2 cup heavy cream
- 3 large eggs
- 1 tablespoon brown sugar
- 1/2 teaspoon vanilla extract
- Salt to taste

Instructions:

1. Preheat the oven to 350°F (175°C).
2. In a bowl, whisk together maple syrup, heavy cream, eggs, brown sugar, vanilla extract, and salt.
3. Stir in crumbled bacon.
4. Pour the mixture into the pre-baked pie crust.
5. Bake for 35-40 minutes until the filling is set and golden. Let cool before serving.

Bourbon Pecan Pie

Ingredients:

- 1 1/2 cups pecans, chopped
- 3/4 cup light corn syrup
- 1/2 cup granulated sugar
- 1/4 cup brown sugar
- 1/4 cup unsalted butter, melted
- 3 large eggs
- 1/4 cup bourbon
- 1 teaspoon vanilla extract
- 1 package pie crust (or homemade crust)

Instructions:

1. Preheat the oven to 350°F (175°C).
2. In a bowl, whisk together corn syrup, sugar, brown sugar, melted butter, eggs, bourbon, and vanilla extract.
3. Stir in the chopped pecans.
4. Pour the filling into the pre-baked pie crust.
5. Bake for 45-50 minutes until the filling is set and the top is golden. Let cool before serving.

Bourbon Chocolate Pecan Pie

Ingredients:

- 1 1/2 cups pecans, chopped
- 1/2 cup semi-sweet chocolate chips
- 1/2 cup light corn syrup
- 1/2 cup brown sugar
- 1/4 cup unsalted butter, melted
- 3 large eggs
- 1/4 cup bourbon
- 1 teaspoon vanilla extract
- 1 package pie crust (or homemade crust)

Instructions:

1. Preheat the oven to 350°F (175°C).
2. In a bowl, whisk together corn syrup, brown sugar, melted butter, eggs, bourbon, and vanilla extract.
3. Stir in pecans and chocolate chips.
4. Pour the mixture into the pre-baked pie crust.
5. Bake for 45-50 minutes until the filling is set and the top is golden. Let cool before serving.

Cinnamon Roll Pie

Ingredients:

- 1 package cinnamon roll dough (store-bought or homemade)
- 1 cup heavy cream
- 1/2 cup granulated sugar
- 2 large eggs
- 1 teaspoon vanilla extract
- 1/4 teaspoon cinnamon
- 1 tablespoon butter, melted

Instructions:

1. Preheat the oven to 350°F (175°C).
2. Unroll the cinnamon roll dough and press it into a pie pan, layering the rolls in a circular pattern.
3. In a bowl, whisk together heavy cream, sugar, eggs, vanilla extract, and cinnamon.
4. Pour the mixture over the cinnamon rolls in the pie pan.
5. Bake for 25-30 minutes until the filling is set and the top is golden.
6. Drizzle with icing from the cinnamon roll package or make your own.

Caramel Apple Pie

Ingredients:

- 6 cups sliced apples (Granny Smith or Honeycrisp)
- 1/2 cup granulated sugar
- 1/4 cup brown sugar
- 1 tablespoon cornstarch
- 1/2 teaspoon cinnamon
- 1/4 teaspoon nutmeg
- 1/2 cup caramel sauce
- 1 tablespoon lemon juice
- 1 package pie crust (or homemade crust)

Instructions:

1. Preheat the oven to 375°F (190°C).
2. In a bowl, toss apples with sugar, brown sugar, cornstarch, cinnamon, nutmeg, and lemon juice.
3. Pour the apple mixture into the pre-baked pie crust.
4. Drizzle caramel sauce over the apples.
5. Top with a second pie crust, crimp the edges, and cut slits for ventilation.
6. Bake for 45-50 minutes until the crust is golden and the filling is bubbly. Let cool before serving.

Chocolate Caramel Pie

Ingredients for Filling:

- 1/2 cup semi-sweet chocolate chips
- 1/2 cup caramel sauce
- 1/2 cup heavy cream
- 1 package pie crust (or homemade crust)

For Topping:

- 1/2 cup whipped cream
- 2 tablespoons caramel sauce

Instructions:

1. Preheat the oven to 350°F (175°C). Bake the pie crust and set aside.
2. In a saucepan, melt the chocolate chips with heavy cream until smooth.
3. Stir in caramel sauce and cook for another 2-3 minutes.
4. Pour the chocolate-caramel filling into the pre-baked pie crust.
5. Refrigerate for at least 4 hours or until set.
6. Top with whipped cream and drizzle with extra caramel sauce before serving.

Apple Pear Pie

Ingredients:

- 3 cups sliced apples (Granny Smith or Honeycrisp)
- 3 cups sliced pears (Bartlett or Bosc)
- 1 cup granulated sugar
- 2 tablespoons cornstarch
- 1 teaspoon cinnamon
- 1 tablespoon lemon juice
- 1 package pie crust (or homemade crust)

Instructions:

1. Preheat the oven to 375°F (190°C).
2. In a bowl, toss apples, pears, sugar, cornstarch, cinnamon, and lemon juice until evenly coated.
3. Pour the mixture into the pre-baked pie crust.
4. Top with a second pie crust, crimp the edges, and cut slits for ventilation.
5. Bake for 45-50 minutes until the crust is golden and the filling is bubbly. Let cool before serving.

Blackberry Pie

Ingredients:

- 4 cups fresh or frozen blackberries
- 1 cup granulated sugar
- 1 tablespoon lemon juice
- 2 tablespoons cornstarch
- 1/4 teaspoon cinnamon
- 1 package pie crust (or homemade crust)

Instructions:

1. Preheat the oven to 375°F (190°C).
2. In a bowl, combine blackberries, sugar, lemon juice, cornstarch, and cinnamon.
3. Roll out the pie crust and place it in a pie pan. Pour the blackberry mixture into the crust.
4. Top with a second crust, crimp the edges, and cut slits in the top for ventilation.
5. Bake for 45-50 minutes until the crust is golden and the filling is bubbly. Let cool before serving.

Pineapple Mango Pie

Ingredients:

- 1 1/2 cups fresh mango, diced
- 1 1/2 cups fresh pineapple, diced
- 3/4 cup granulated sugar
- 1 tablespoon cornstarch
- 1 tablespoon lemon juice
- 1 package pie crust (or homemade crust)

Instructions:

1. Preheat the oven to 375°F (190°C).
2. In a bowl, combine mango, pineapple, sugar, cornstarch, and lemon juice.
3. Pour the fruit mixture into the pre-baked pie crust.
4. Top with a second crust, crimp the edges, and cut slits in the top for ventilation.
5. Bake for 45-50 minutes until the crust is golden and the filling is bubbly. Let cool before serving.

Pear Ginger Pie

Ingredients:

- 4 cups fresh pears, peeled and sliced
- 1 tablespoon grated fresh ginger
- 1/2 cup granulated sugar
- 1 tablespoon lemon juice
- 2 tablespoons cornstarch
- 1 teaspoon cinnamon
- 1/4 teaspoon nutmeg
- 1 package pie crust (or homemade crust)

Instructions:

1. Preheat the oven to 375°F (190°C).
2. In a bowl, toss the sliced pears with grated ginger, sugar, lemon juice, cornstarch, cinnamon, and nutmeg until evenly coated.
3. Roll out the pie crust and place it in a pie pan. Pour the pear mixture into the crust.
4. Top with a second pie crust, crimp the edges, and cut slits in the top for ventilation.
5. Bake for 45-50 minutes until the crust is golden and the filling is bubbly. Let cool before serving.

Lime Coconut Pie

Ingredients:

- 1 can (14 oz) sweetened condensed milk
- 1/2 cup fresh lime juice
- 1/2 cup shredded coconut
- 3 large eggs
- 1 tablespoon lime zest
- 1 package graham cracker crust

Instructions:

1. Preheat the oven to 350°F (175°C).
2. In a bowl, whisk together sweetened condensed milk, lime juice, eggs, lime zest, and shredded coconut.
3. Pour the mixture into the graham cracker crust.
4. Bake for 25-30 minutes until the filling is set and golden.
5. Let cool and refrigerate for at least 2 hours before serving.

Chiffon Pie

Ingredients for Filling:

- 1 cup fruit puree (lemon, orange, or berry)
- 3/4 cup granulated sugar
- 3 large egg yolks
- 1 teaspoon unflavored gelatin
- 1/4 cup cold water
- 1 cup heavy cream, whipped
- 1 teaspoon vanilla extract
- 1 pre-baked pie crust

Instructions:

1. In a saucepan, combine fruit puree, sugar, and egg yolks. Cook over medium heat until thickened.
2. Dissolve gelatin in cold water and stir into the mixture. Remove from heat and let cool to room temperature.
3. Gently fold in the whipped cream and vanilla extract.
4. Pour the filling into the pre-baked pie crust and refrigerate for at least 4 hours until set.
5. Serve chilled with additional whipped cream if desired.

Chocolate Hazelnut Pie

Ingredients:

- 1 pre-baked pie crust
- 1 cup milk chocolate chips
- 1/2 cup hazelnut spread (like Nutella)
- 1/2 cup heavy cream
- 1/4 cup granulated sugar
- 1 teaspoon vanilla extract
- 1/2 cup toasted hazelnuts, chopped

Instructions:

1. Preheat the oven to 350°F (175°C). In a saucepan, melt the chocolate chips and hazelnut spread with heavy cream over low heat, stirring constantly.
2. Stir in sugar and vanilla extract, cooking for 1-2 minutes until smooth.
3. Pour the mixture into the pre-baked pie crust.
4. Bake for 15-20 minutes until the filling is set.
5. Let cool before topping with chopped toasted hazelnuts. Refrigerate for at least 2 hours before serving.

Cranberry Orange Pie

Ingredients:

- 2 cups fresh cranberries
- 1/2 cup orange juice
- 1 tablespoon orange zest
- 1/2 cup granulated sugar
- 2 tablespoons cornstarch
- 1/4 teaspoon cinnamon
- 1 package pie crust (or homemade crust)

Instructions:

1. Preheat the oven to 375°F (190°C).
2. In a saucepan, combine cranberries, orange juice, orange zest, sugar, cornstarch, and cinnamon. Cook over medium heat until the cranberries burst and the mixture thickens.
3. Pour the cranberry-orange mixture into the pre-baked pie crust.
4. Top with a second crust, crimp the edges, and cut slits for ventilation.
5. Bake for 45-50 minutes until the crust is golden and the filling is bubbly. Let cool before serving.

Spiced Pear Pie

Ingredients:

- 4 cups fresh pears, peeled and sliced
- 3/4 cup granulated sugar
- 1 tablespoon lemon juice
- 2 tablespoons cornstarch
- 1 teaspoon cinnamon
- 1/4 teaspoon nutmeg
- 1/4 teaspoon ginger
- 1 package pie crust (or homemade crust)

Instructions:

1. Preheat the oven to 375°F (190°C).
2. In a bowl, mix sliced pears, sugar, lemon juice, cornstarch, cinnamon, nutmeg, and ginger.
3. Roll out the pie crust and place it in a pie pan. Pour the pear mixture into the crust.
4. Top with a second pie crust, crimp the edges, and cut slits for ventilation.
5. Bake for 45-50 minutes until the crust is golden and the filling is bubbly. Let cool before serving.

Chocolate Almond Pie

Ingredients:

- 1 cup semi-sweet chocolate chips
- 1/2 cup almond butter
- 1/2 cup heavy cream
- 1/2 cup granulated sugar
- 3 large eggs
- 1 teaspoon vanilla extract
- 1 pre-baked pie crust
- 1/4 cup sliced almonds for garnish

Instructions:

1. Preheat the oven to 350°F (175°C). In a saucepan, melt chocolate chips, almond butter, and heavy cream over low heat.
2. In a bowl, whisk together sugar, eggs, and vanilla extract.
3. Stir the melted chocolate mixture into the egg mixture and pour into the pre-baked pie crust.
4. Bake for 25-30 minutes until the filling is set.
5. Let cool before garnishing with sliced almonds. Refrigerate for at least 2 hours before serving.

Butterscotch Pie

Ingredients:

- 1 cup brown sugar
- 1/4 cup cornstarch
- 1/4 teaspoon salt
- 2 1/2 cups whole milk
- 4 large egg yolks
- 2 tablespoons unsalted butter
- 1 teaspoon vanilla extract
- 1 pre-baked pie crust

Instructions:

1. Preheat the oven to 350°F (175°C). In a saucepan, combine brown sugar, cornstarch, and salt. Gradually whisk in the milk.
2. Cook over medium heat until thickened, stirring constantly.
3. Beat the egg yolks and slowly add a little of the hot mixture to temper them. Add the egg mixture back to the saucepan and cook for 2-3 minutes.
4. Stir in butter and vanilla extract.
5. Pour the butterscotch filling into the pre-baked pie crust and bake for 10 minutes.
6. Let cool before serving. Optionally, top with whipped cream.